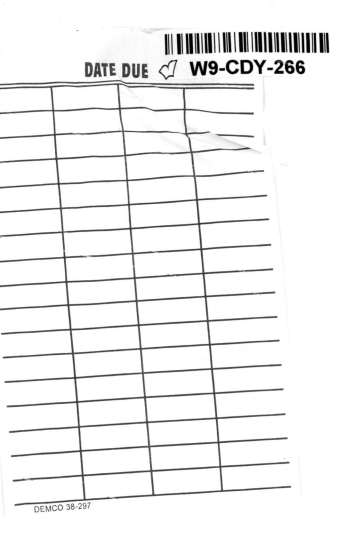
W9-CDY-266

BASEBALL
FOR FUN!

By Sandra Will

Content Adviser: Clay Weiner, Writer and Player/Coach, Brooklyn, New York
Reading Adviser: Frances J. Bonacci, Reading Specialist, Cambridge, Massachusetts

COMPASS POINT BOOKS

MINNEAPOLIS, MINNESOTA

Compass Point Books
3109 West 50th Street, #115
Minneapolis, MN 55410

Visit Compass Point Books on the Internet at *www.compasspointbooks.com*
or e-mail your request to *custserv@compasspointbooks.com*

Photographs ©: Zoran Milich/Getty Images, front cover (left); Artville, front cover (right), 25 (right); PhotoDisc, 4, 12 (right), 36–37, 42 (top right), 43 (top left), 45 (top); Courtesy of Rawlings, 5, 12 (left), 13, 43 (bottom left), 45 (bottom); Christie K. Silver, 13 (bottom left); Otto Gruele Jr./Getty Images, 6–7, 37; Brian Bahr/Getty Images, 8–9, 10–11, 34–35; Ezra Shaw/Getty Images, 14–15; Library of Congress, 15, 33, 38, 40–41, 42; Stephen Dunn/Getty Images, 17, 28–29; Todd Rosenberg/Getty Images, 19; Corel, 20, 44; Al Bello/Getty Images, 22–23; ArtToday, 23, 32; Eliot Schechter/Getty Images, 25 (left); Tom Hauck/Getty Images, 26–27; Doug Pensinger/Getty Images, 27; Elsa Hasch/Getty Images, 30–31; Jed Jacobsohn/Getty Images, 39; Rick Stewart/Getty Images, 43 (center bottom); Matthew Stockman/Getty Images, 43 (bottom right); Carin Krasner/Getty Images, 44–45.

Editors: Ryan Blitstein/Bill SMITH STUDIO and Catherine Neitge
Photo Researchers: Christie Silver and Sandra Will/Bill SMITH STUDIO
Designer: Jay Jaffe/Bill SMITH STUDIO

Library of Congress Cataloging-in-Publication Data
Will, Sandra.
    Baseball for fun / by Sandra Will.
    p. cm. — (Sports for fun)
    Summary: Describes the basic rules, skills, and important people and events in the sport of baseball.
    Includes bibliographical references (p.   ) and index.
    ISBN 0-7565-0428-7 (hardcover)
    1. Baseball—Juvenile literature. [1. Baseball.] I. Title. II. Series.
    GV867.4.W55 2003
    796.357—dc21   2002015120

Table of Contents

Ground Rules

Playing the Game

People, Places, and Fun

Note: In this book, there are two kinds of vocabulary words. Baseball Words to Know are words specific to baseball. They are in **bold** and are defined on page 46. Other Words to Know are helpful words that aren't related only to baseball. They are in ***bold and italicized***. These are defined on page 47.

Spring Is for Baseball!

Have you ever played baseball? In the spring, people of all ages play baseball in parks, fields, and stadiums. Baseball is like many older bat-and-ball games, such as rounders. The modern game of baseball started in America and spread around the world. The games of T-ball and softball also came from baseball. Baseball is the official national sport of the United States.

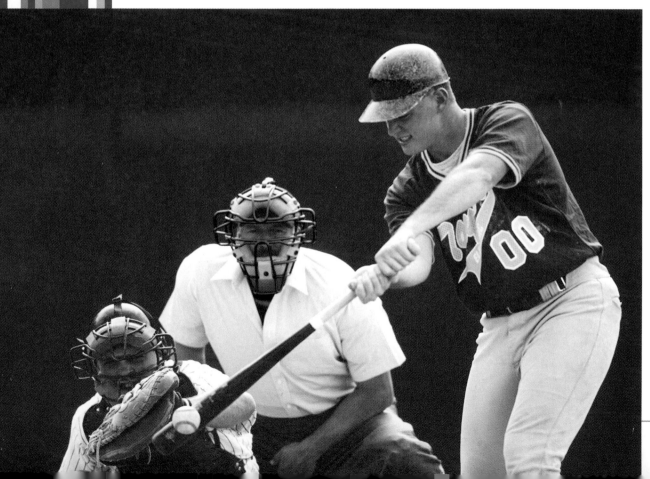

Goal of the Game

Baseball is a team sport. The object of the game is to score more **runs**, or points, than the other team. A team scores runs by hitting the ball, running between the bases, and reaching home plate. The other team tries to keep players from scoring by making **outs** (see p. 8).

A baseball only weighs about 5 ounces [140 grams], but it has a unique design. Horsehide strips are on the outside. Cotton thread, rubber, woolen yarn, and a cork in the center are inside.

On the Diamond

Baseball fields have an infield and an outfield. The infield has a home plate, three bases, and a pitcher's mound. A distance of ninety feet (twenty-seven meters) separates each base. The layout of the infield makes a ninety-foot diamond. The baseline is the three-foot (one-meter) area on both sides of the imaginary line that connects the bases. The outfield is the rest of the field between the infield and the outfield fence. Look at the picture to learn the names of the parts of the baseball field.

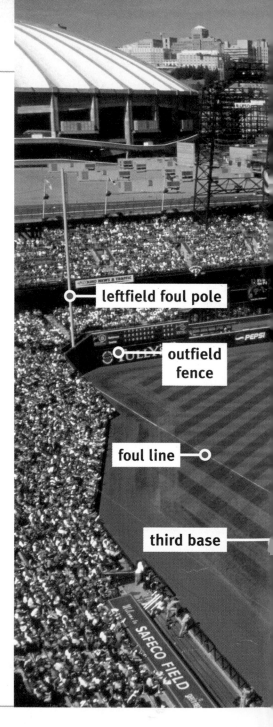

leftfield foul pole

outfield fence

foul line

third base

SAFECO FIELD

How do you know if a ball is playable?

The foul lines show if a ball is hit in **fair territory**. They run from home plate down the baselines into the outfield. Yellow posts called foul poles mark the foul line at the outfield fence. A batter can't get a hit from a ball hit foul. But if a fielder catches a **fly ball** in **foul territory**, the batter is out!

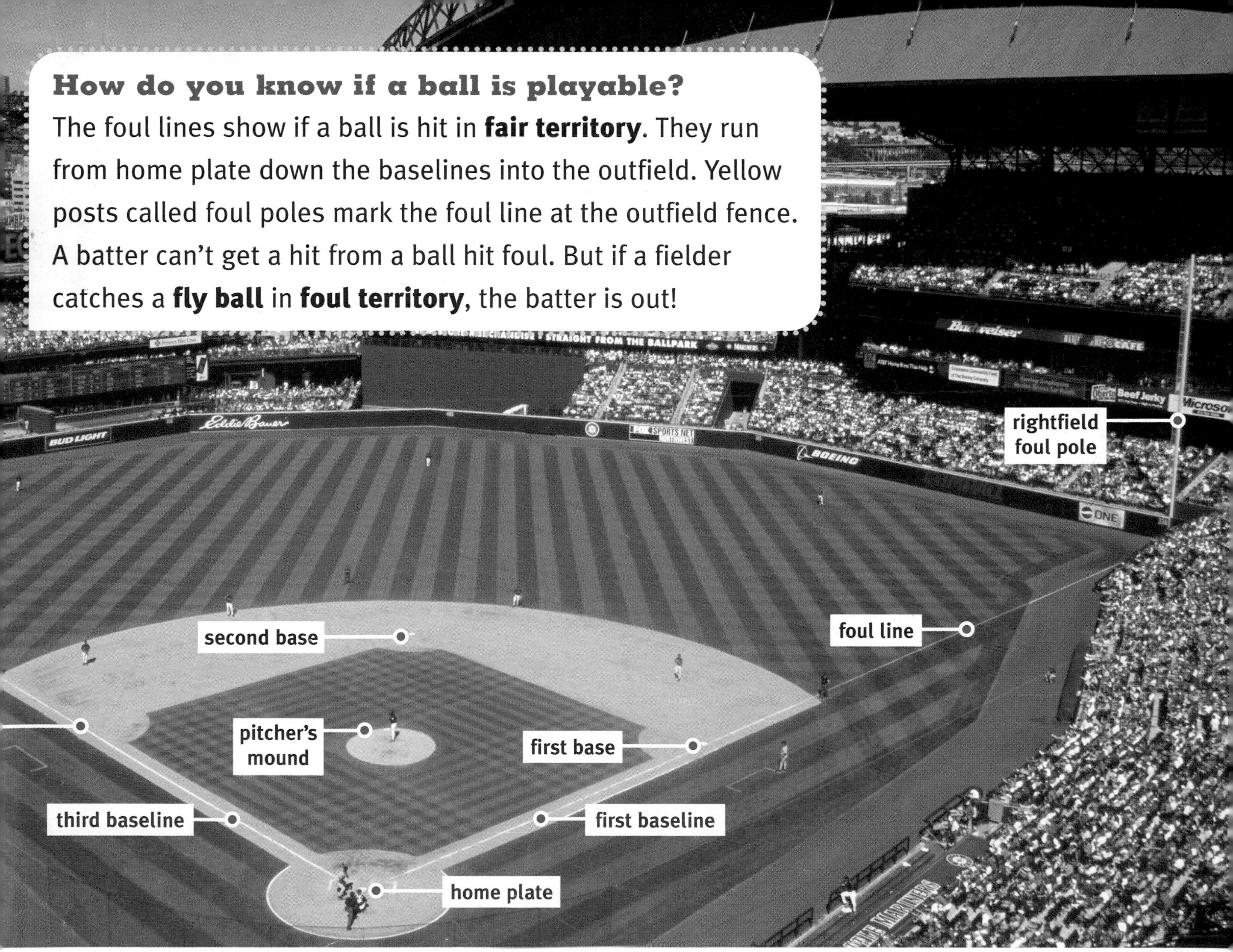

rightfield foul pole

second base

foul line

pitcher's mound

first base

third baseline

first baseline

home plate

Taking the Field

A baseball game is divided into nine **innings**. In the first part of the inning, or top, the home team takes the field and plays **defense**. The visiting team is up to bat on **offense**. The offensive players wait in the dugout for their turn to bat. The dugouts are located along the first and third baselines. When the home team makes three outs (see table), the teams switch places. In the last part of the inning, or bottom, the home team bats, and the visiting team plays defense.

You're Out!

A player can be called out in many ways.

HOW?	DESCRIPTION
Strikeout	A batter is called out when he has three strikes (see p. 20).
Thrown out	A batter hits a ground ball, and a fielder throws him out at first base.
Fly out	A fielder catches a fly ball before it touches the ground.
Tagged out	A fielder touches a base runner with the ball when he is not on base.

Hit 'em Home

A team scores one run when a player safely runs all of the bases and crosses home plate. Hitting a **home run** is the fastest way to score. A home run is a fair ball hit over the outfield fence. **Base hits** allow runners to reach base. Singles, doubles, and triples are base hits that advance batters to first, second, or third base. A batter earns a **run batted in (RBI)** if a base runner scores as a result of his or her at-bat.

Barry Bonds of the San Francisco Giants slugged seventy-three homers in 2001, breaking Mark McGwire's record.

Grand Slam

When runners are on first, second, and third bases, the bases are loaded. A home run with the bases loaded is called a **grand slam**. Baseball fans have a special nickname for the grand slam: the "grand salami."

Suit Up

Imagine a solid ball traveling 100 miles (161 kilometers) per hour at your head! Baseball requires special equipment that protects players from injury and helps them play the game.

Baseball uniforms have four parts: short-sleeved shirt, pants with a belt, stirrup socks, and a cap.

Bats come in different lengths and sizes. Baseball bats are made of *aluminum* or wood. In professional leagues, only wooden bats are allowed.

Hard plastic helmets lined with foam protect a player's head while he or she bats and runs the bases.

Gloves called mitts allow players to field and catch the ball without hurting their hands. All defensive players wear mitts, but some positions have special types of gloves (see right).

Batting gloves help players grip the bat and protect a batter's hands from blisters.

Special shoes called cleats give players more traction.

Catching On

Catchers wear a special mitt, a mask, shin guards, and padding to shield them from wild pitches, foul balls, and (sometimes) broken bats.

Play Ball!

Baseball is a game with many *traditions*. Before the start of each game, the national anthems of the teams play while fans and players sing along. A famous person or local hero often throws out the first pitch. The game officially begins when the umpire yells, "Play ball!" During the middle of the seventh inning in many ballparks, fans stand and sing "Take Me Out To The Ball Game." This is known as the seventh-inning stretch.

First Pitch of the Year

President Woodrow Wilson threw out the first pitch on Opening Day of the 1916 baseball season. The tradition of throwing out the first pitch was started by President William Howard Taft in 1910.

The Lineup

The lineup is the group of nine players that bat for each team. Team managers, or coaches, put their hitters into a numbered batting order.

The first batter in the lineup is the leadoff hitter. The leadoff hitter gets base hits often and is a fast runner. The second batter should also be a good hitter. The third, fourth, and fifth spots are called the heart of the order. They are the hardest hitters on the team. The fourth batter is the cleanup hitter because he can "clean" the bases with a big hit.

The sixth, seventh, eighth, and ninth places in the lineup are known as the bottom of the order. Batters in the bottom of the order are usually the weakest hitters. However, even these players must hit well and produce runs.

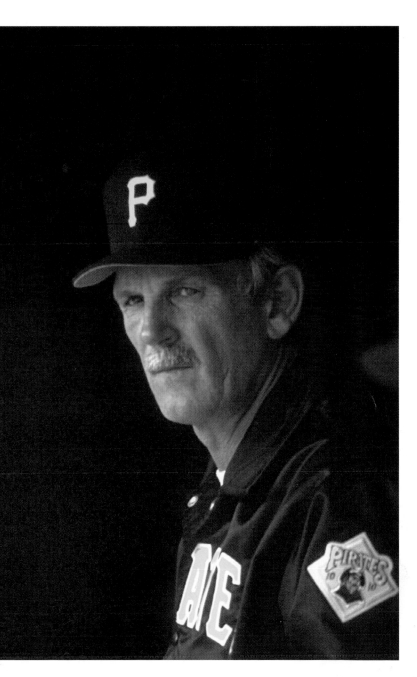

The lineup card lists the batting order as well as players who might be put in later in the game.

Play Catch

Infielders and outfielders work together to prevent the offensive team from scoring.

First Base (1B): The first baseman catches most balls thrown by other infielders. A good first baseman *prevents* **errors** made by other infielders by scooping up in-the-dirt throws.

Second Base (2B): The second baseman is very important in making a **double play** (see p. 34). The second baseman also makes **relay** throws from the outfield to third base and home plate.

Third Base (3B): Third base is called the "hot corner" because hits travel at the fastest speeds toward this position. The third baseman must be able to react quickly. **Line drives** (fly balls that travel straight through the air) move fast.

Shortstop (SS): The shortstop fields more ground balls and line drives than any other position. A shortstop must be able to field and throw the ball quickly.

Outfielders: The Right Fielder (RF), Left Fielder (LF), and Center Fielder (CF) work together to prevent base hits. The right fielder often has the strongest throwing arm. The center fielder is usually the fastest runner.

Pitcher (P): Along with facing batters, pitchers must be ready to field the ball. The pitcher must also cover first base when the first baseman fields a ball.

Catcher (C): Catchers go after fly balls hit behind home plate. They also throw out runners trying to steal bases.

In the Zone

When a batter swings at a pitch and misses, he earns a strike. The **strike zone** is the area over home plate between the middle of the batter's chest and the bottom of the knees. An official called an **umpire** stands behind the plate. If a pitcher throws the ball in the strike zone and the batter doesn't swing, the umpire calls a strike on the batter. A batter is allowed three strikes before being called out.

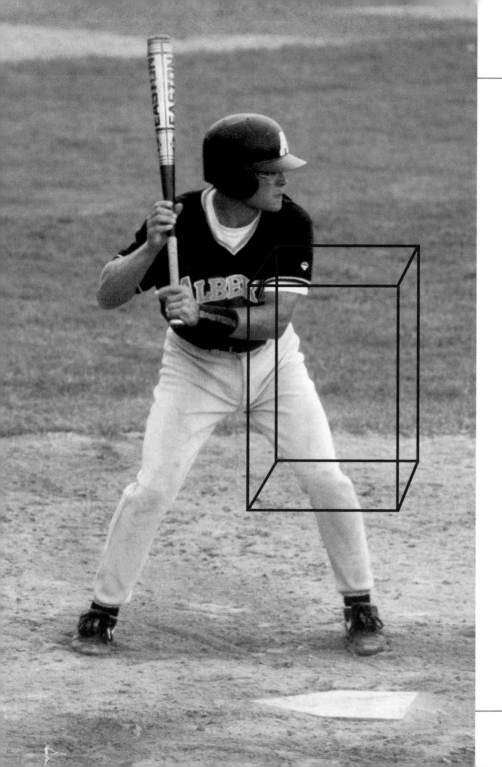

Take Your Base

If a pitch is outside the strike zone and the batter doesn't swing, it's called a **ball**. A batter gets a free trip to first base when he or she has four balls. This is called a **base on balls (BB)** or a walk. The batter also gets a walk if he or she is hit by a pitch. Until 1889, a hitter had to have nine balls to walk to first!

Can You Count?

Umpires keep track of the batter's **count,** or number of balls and strikes.

What is a 3-2 count? Three balls and two strikes.

Stealing Second

Smart baserunning is important. **Base runners** steal bases to move into **scoring position** (standing on second or third base). When a runner wants to steal a base, he or she waits for the pitcher to release the ball. Then, the runner tries to make it to the next base without being thrown out by the catcher. A good base runner must be able to run fast. Coaches sometimes replace a slower runner with a faster pinch runner.

Be Careful!

Sometimes a runner gets stuck in a pickle between two bases. He or she is caught between two defensive players, and one has the ball.

Perfect Pitch

It's a simple fact: great pitching beats great hitting. If two or three batters are having a bad day, a team can still play well enough to win. If a pitcher has one bad inning, his or her team could be in trouble. Pitchers use a *variety* of pitches to strike out batters. For each pitch, the pitcher grips the ball in a different way. Here are some of the common pitches used in baseball:

PITCH NAMES	DESCRIPTION	GRIP
Fastball	a very fast pitch that comes straight across the plate	
Curveball	a pitch that curves up, down, or to one side as it nears the plate	
Change Up	a slow pitch that throws off a batter's timing	

The Bullpen

What do bulls have to do with baseball? Pitchers who are not playing in the game sit in the bullpen. When the starting pitcher gets tired, the manager calls in a relief pitcher. He sometimes calls in a left-handed pitcher, or "southpaw," to throw against a right-handed batter.

Did You Know?

The average baseball lasts only six pitches in a major league game!

I Got It!

Fielders need to pay attention to where they stand. When a fielder tags or throws a base runner out, it is called a **putout**. To make a putout, a fielder has to be in the right spot. Fielders play shallow (closer to the plate) or deep (farther from the plate).

Sometimes many fielders go after the same fly ball. To avoid a *collision*, fielders call the ball so they know who is making the play. They call it by yelling or waving their hands.

The Cutoff Man

Before the ball is hit, an outfielder needs to know where to throw the ball if it comes to him. The outfielder throws to the cutoff man (usually the second baseman or shortstop). The cutoff man makes a relay throw to try to get the runner out.

New York Yankees second baseman Alfonso Soriano makes a relay throw.

Lay It on the Line

A bunt is a special type of hit. When batters bunt, they push the ball softly with their bat. A well-bunted ball stays in the shallow part of the infield. Batters often try to place a bunt down a baseline.

Switch!

Along with special types of hits, managers also use special hitters. A **switch hitter** can hit from the right or left side. A pinch hitter takes the place of a weaker batter late in the game.

There are three types of bunts used in baseball. A drag bunt is a bunt where the hitter is trying to get on base. Sacrifice bunts advance a base runner, but the batter is usually thrown out. In a squeeze play, the batter bunts to score a runner from third base.

Follow the Rules

Baseball is a game with many rules. It would be tough to learn them all, but it is important for a player to know as many as he or she can.

- On fly balls, the runner can tag up, or wait on the base until the ball is caught. After the ball is caught, the runner can run to the next base.

- When runners are on base with fewer than two outs, defensive players must follow the infield fly rule. An infield fly is a fair fly ball that can be caught by an infielder. Defensive players cannot let the ball drop to try and throw runners out. The batter is automatically out, and the base runners keep their bases.

- If a base runner runs outside of the baseline, he or she is out.

- If the teams have the same number of runs after nine innings, the game is tied. The game goes into extra innings until one team has a lead at the end of an inning.

- If a base runner is hit by a fair ball while running between bases, he or she is out.

- When the catcher drops the ball on the third strike, he or she must tag the batter or throw him out at first. This is called the three strike rule.

- If a batter bunts in foul territory with two strikes, he is out.

When tagging up, the base runner doesn't watch the outfielder catch the ball. The coach tells him when to start running.

Head Games

Baseball is about more than just throwing, fielding, and hitting. Players have to think, too. Teams use offensive *strategies* to win games.

• Coaches use hand signals to tell the players what to do. The third base coach tells the batter how he or she is supposed to hit on each pitch. The signals also tell the base runner what type of play is coming.

- A sacrifice fly is a fly ball caught deep in the outfield. A runner tags up on third base and reaches home safely. The batter sacrifices himself to score the run.

- In some leagues, not all defensive players bat. A designated hitter (DH) bats in the lineup but does not play defense. DHs take the place of the pitcher, who is usually a weak hitter. In leagues where DHs aren't allowed, the manager makes a tough decision. Should he send in a pinch hitter for the pitcher late in the game? If the pitcher is pitching well, taking him out might mean the other team will score more runs. However, most pitchers aren't great hitters. A pinch hitter might help his own team score.

John McGraw was one of the great master strategists of baseball. He spent thirty-one years with the New York Giants in the early 1900s. McGraw thought up many strategies that teams still use today.

Turning Two

Strategies are also important on defense. A smart defensive player knows what to do on every play.

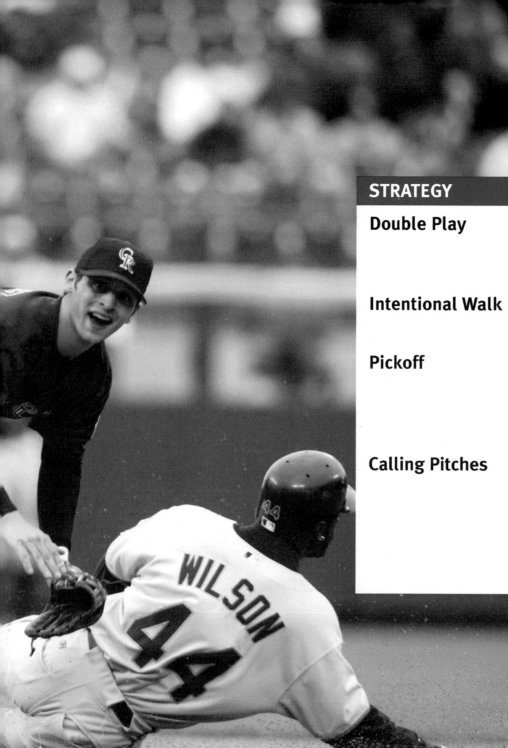

STRATEGY	DESCRIPTION
Double Play	The defense makes two outs on one hit ball. The double play is also called "turning two."
Intentional Walk	The pitcher walks a dangerous batter on purpose.
Pickoff	The pitcher throws to first base instead of home. The pitcher uses the pickoff to stop runners from stealing bases.
Calling Pitches	Pitchers and catchers have a special code. The catcher calls pitches by moving his or her fingers. The pitcher sees the catcher's fingers and knows what pitch to throw.

The Big Leagues

America has one main *professional* organization known as Major League Baseball (MLB). MLB has two leagues, totaling 30 teams: the National League (NL) and the American League (AL). All teams in MLB have professional minor league teams that train young players.

In the past, there were other organized baseball leagues. Until 1947, MLB excluded African-American players from its teams. African-Americans formed their own leagues, called Negro Leagues. Chicago Cubs owner Philip Wrigley formed the All-American Girls Baseball League (AAGBL) in 1943. The AAGBL played its last season in 1954.

Going Global

Baseball is a worldwide sport. More than 100 teams are part of the International Baseball Federation (IBF).

A few of the best players from outside America have come to play in MLB. One of them is Ichiro Suzuki, the Seattle Mariners' speedy right fielder, from Japan.

Legends

Thousands of players have contributed to baseball's rich history. Jackie Robinson and Cal Ripken Jr. are two of the best.

Jackie Robinson

Jackie Robinson joined the Brooklyn Dodgers in 1947, becoming Major League Baseball's first African-American player. He was born in Cairo, Georgia, on January 31, 1919. Robinson was a star at UCLA before he went on to play in the Negro and Major Leagues. During his ten seasons with the Dodgers, he led the team to six pennant titles. Because of his courage and fantastic baseball skills, Jackie Robinson changed the face of baseball. He died in 1972.

Calvin (Cal) Ripken Jr.

Cal Ripken spent his entire major league career as a shortstop and third baseman for the Baltimore Orioles. He was born August 24, 1960, in Havre de Grace, Maryland. In 1982, Ripken was voted the American League Rookie of the Year. He holds the world record for **consecutive** games played: 2,632. Ripken didn't miss a game from May 1982 to September 1998. Ripken was selected to nineteen All-Star games during his career. Known as excellent, dependable, and consistent, Cal Ripken was a leader on and off the field until he retired in 2001.

The Fall Classic

The World Series started all the way back in 1892. From 1892 to 1900, the best National League teams competed in four "World's Championship Series." The first modern World Series was in 1903, when the AL's Boston Pilgrims played against the NL's Pittsburgh Pirates.

The World Series is a best-of-seven game series. The first team to win four games is the champion.

The final game of the 1905 World Series at the Polo Grounds in New York City. The New York Giants beat the Philadelphia Athletics.

The Best of the Best

The New York Yankees have dominated the World Series more than any other team. The Yankees, known as the "Bronx Bombers," have appeared in thirty-seven World Series and won twenty-six times. The Yankees are the only MLB team to win four consecutive World Series (1936–1939) and the only to win five consecutive World Series (1949–1953).

What Happened When?

1823 **1860** **1870** **1880** **1890** **1900** **1910** **1920** **1930**

1823 The earliest baseball match was recorded in New York City.

1856 Baseball becomes known as America's national pastime.

1858 Baseball's first admission (fifty cents) is charged for an all-star game.

1869 The Cincinnati Red Stockings become the first professional team.

1876 Eight teams form the National League.

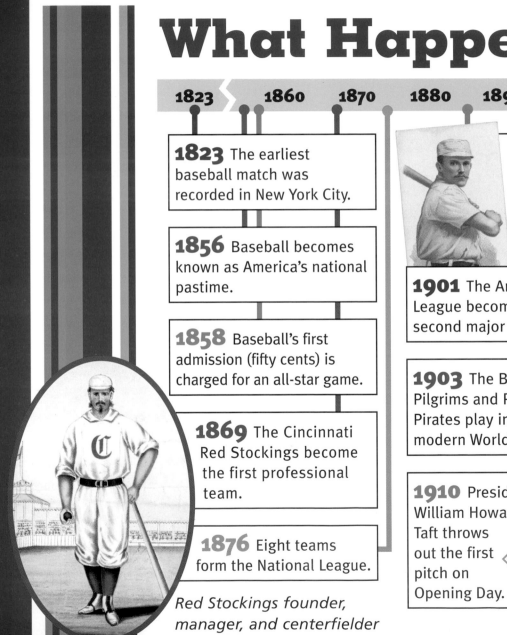

Red Stockings founder, manager, and centerfielder Harry Wright

1880s The first baseball cards appear.

1901 The American League becomes the second major league.

1903 The Boston Pilgrims and Pittsburgh Pirates play in the first modern World Series.

1910 President William Howard Taft throws out the first pitch on Opening Day.

1921 Americans enjoy baseball at home with the first radio broadcast of a major league game.

1927 Babe Ruth becomes the first player to hit sixty home runs in a single season.

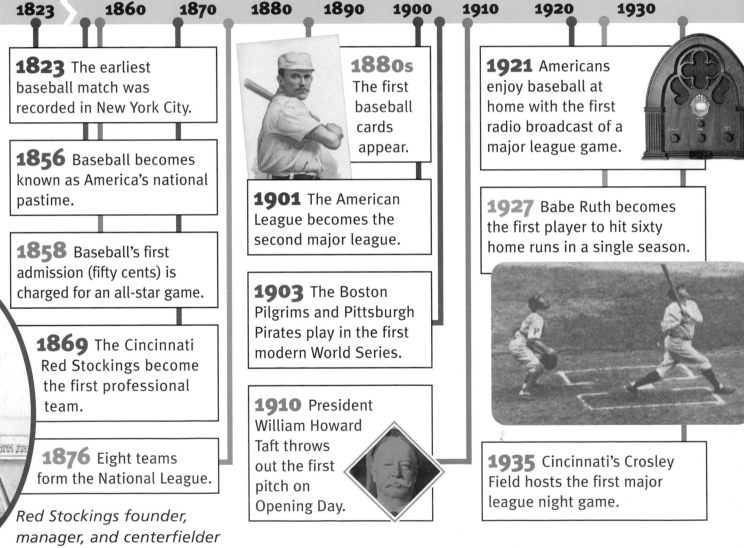

1935 Cincinnati's Crosley Field hosts the first major league night game.

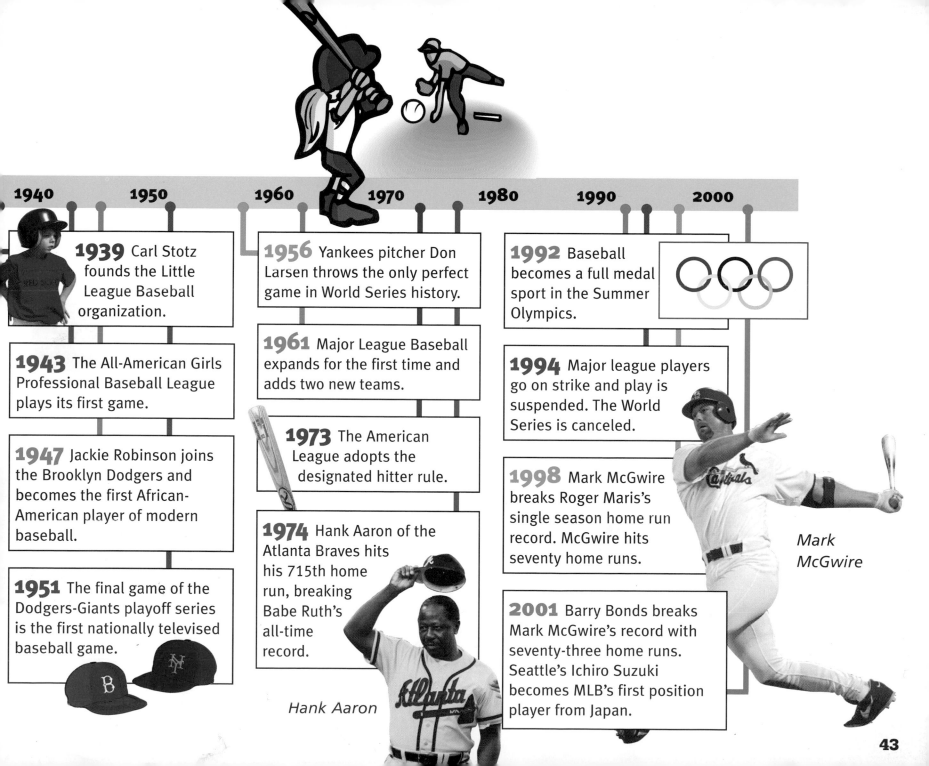

1940   **1950**   **1960**   **1970**   **1980**   **1990**   **2000**

1939 Carl Stotz founds the Little League Baseball organization.

1943 The All-American Girls Professional Baseball League plays its first game.

1947 Jackie Robinson joins the Brooklyn Dodgers and becomes the first African-American player of modern baseball.

1951 The final game of the Dodgers-Giants playoff series is the first nationally televised baseball game.

1956 Yankees pitcher Don Larsen throws the only perfect game in World Series history.

1961 Major League Baseball expands for the first time and adds two new teams.

1973 The American League adopts the designated hitter rule.

1974 Hank Aaron of the Atlanta Braves hits his 715th home run, breaking Babe Ruth's all-time record.

Hank Aaron

1992 Baseball becomes a full medal sport in the Summer Olympics.

1994 Major league players go on strike and play is suspended. The World Series is canceled.

1998 Mark McGwire breaks Roger Maris's single season home run record. McGwire hits seventy home runs.

2001 Barry Bonds breaks Mark McGwire's record with seventy-three home runs. Seattle's Ichiro Suzuki becomes MLB's first position player from Japan.

Mark McGwire

43

Baseball Bonanza

The Skydome is the home of the Toronto Blue Jays. It was the first stadium with a **retractable** roof. If the weather is too cold or too rainy, they just close the dome!

The first catcher's mask was based on a fencing mask. Harvard Baseball Club captain Fred Thayer invented the catcher's mask in 1877.

An easy-to-catch fly ball is called a can of corn.

CORN

Fans prefer dogs! In the early 1900s, ice cream sales were low during the cool months of the season. Harry M. Stevens decided to sell hot dogs at games. Today, hot dogs are the most popular food at ballparks.

The Chicago Cubs installed the first ballpark organ in 1941. Baseball organs are used to play songs like "Take Me Out To The Ball Game" during the seventh-inning stretch.

Teams "retire" jersey numbers to honor their best players. Once a number is retired, no other player can wear it.

There are hundreds of nicknames for a home run. Here are a few: big fly, big tomato, blast, bonk, crack, dinger, four-bagger, granny, gopher ball, homer, knock, long ball, moon shot, round-tripper, smash, tater, and whack.

Baseball Words to Know

ball: a pitch that the home plate umpire judges to be outside of the strike zone

base hit: a hit that lets a runner reach base safely

base on balls (also called a walk): a runner gets four balls in his turn at bat and he advances to first base

base runner: an offensive player who reaches base safely

bases loaded: runners on first, second, and third base

batter: the player on the offensive team who is at the plate taking his turn to bat

count: the number of balls and strikes on the batter at any time

defense: when the team is trying to stop the offense from scoring

double play: two outs on the same play

error: a defensive player makes a mistake while fielding the ball

fair territory: the area inside the foul lines

fly ball: a ball that is hit into the air

foul territory: the area outside the foul lines

grand slam: a home run with the bases loaded

ground ball (grounder): a hit that bounces off the ground

home run: a four-base hit where the batter and all base runners score

inning: a part of a baseball game consisting of a turn at bat for each team

intentional walk: the pitcher walks the batter on purpose

line drive: a batted ball that is hit hard in the air in a straight line

offense: when the team is trying to score runs

on deck: the hitter up next for a turn at bat

out: not successful in reaching a base

putout: the act of getting an offensive player out

relay: a throw from one fielder to another, who then throws the ball to a third player

run: a point

run batted in: a player earns one when a teammate scores during his at-bat

scoring position: a runner on second or third base is in scoring position

strikeout: a batter is called out after three strikes

strike zone: the area over home plate between a batter's shoulder and knees

switch hitter: a player who can hit from both sides of the plate—right-handed or left-handed

umpire: the official who enforces baseball's rules

Metric Conversion
1 yard = .9144 meters

Other Words to Know

Here are definitions for some of the words used in this book:

aluminum: a type of metal

collision: when two things run into each other

consecutive: in a row, without stopping

prevent: to stop from happening

professional: a person paid to do a job or play a game

retractable: able to be pulled back

strategy: a plan or method to do something

tradition: a practice that people pass down from generation to generation

variety: many different kinds

Where To Learn More

AT THE LIBRARY

Kasoff, Jerry. *Baseball Just for Kids: Skill, Strategies and Stories to Make You a Better Ballplayer*. Englewood Cliffs, NJ: Grand Slam Press, Inc., 1996.

Gutman, Dan. *Baseball's Biggest Bloopers: The Games That Got Away*. New York: Puffin, 1995.

Christopher, Matt, and S. Peters, ed. *Great Moments in Baseball History*. New York: Little Brown & Co., 1996.

ON THE ROAD

National Baseball Hall of Fame and Museum
25 Main Street
P.O. Box 590
Cooperstown, NY 13326
607/547-7200
http://www.baseballhalloffame.org

Negro Leagues Baseball Museum
1616 E. 18th Street
Kansas City, MO 64108-1610
816/221-1920
http://www.nlbm.com

ON THE WEB

Major League Baseball
http://www.mlb.com

Minor League Baseball
http://www.minorleaguebaseball.com

National Collegiate Athletic Association Baseball
http://www.ncaa.org

International Baseball Federation
http://www.baseball.ch

Little League Baseball
http://www.littleleague.org

INDEX

ABOUT THE AUTHOR

Sandra Will graduated magna cum laude from Barnard College, Columbia University with a B.A. degree in English Literature. An avid Yankees fan, Sandra's passion for baseball (and sports in general) stems from her grandfather, who was a professional baseball player in the 1920s and 1930s. Originally from Chehalis, Washington, Sandra lives in New York City.